name is

BOOK

JOHN AGARD

illustrated by

NEIL PACKER

WALKER BOOKS
AND SUBSIDIARIES
LONDON · BOSTON · SYDNEY · AUCKLAND

To Caroline Royds, Alice Horrocks and Beth Aves
for editorial nurturing and design,
to Neil Packer for the visual grooming and
to Eddie Burnett who gave up boxing for books

First published 2014 by Walker Books Ltd
87 Vauxhall Walk, London SE11 5HJ

This edition published 2016

2 4 6 8 10 9 7 5 3 1

Text © 2014 John Agard
Illustrations © 2014 Neil Packer

This book has been typeset in Brioso Pro and BlissIcelandic

Printed and bound in Great Britain by Clays Ltd, St Ives plc

British Library Cataloguing in Publication Data:
a catalogue for this book is available from the British Library

ISBN 978-1-4063-6898-7

www.walker.co.uk

Remembering

WENDY BOASE
(1944–1999)

who supported the idea

of *My Name Is Book* in its infancy

two decades ago

Contents

MY
NAME
IS
BOOK

and I'll tell you

the story of

my life.

In good time you'll be hearing about clay
tablets, the invention of the alphabet,

parchment, manuscripts that light up, libraries and all that kind of stuff. But my story goes even further back.

Before Book,

there was

Breath.

By firelight people sang songs and told stories. They chanted while dancing to honour the seasons. And the old ones passed on the old ways to the young by

word of mouth. By the power of memory.
Yes, people kept me in their heads and
told me with their lips.

Writing was not yet born.

If you don't know the trees
you may be lost in the forest,
but if you don't know the stories
you may be lost in life.

Siberian elder

The Whodunnit of Writing

Many people
believe that writing began

more than five thousand years ago with the Sumerians of ancient Mesopotamia, now modern Iraq.

It might have been invented by a Sumerian farmer who just happened to be doodling with clay on the banks of the River Tigris or the Euphrates. Well, not exactly doodling, but putting marks on clay to keep check of his cattle and barley. Or a Sumerian woman might have been decorating her clay pots, and one thing led to another. Who knows?

It's also possible that writing began a

few hundred years before then with the ancient Egyptians, or maybe even earlier with the Harappan civilization of the Indus Valley, in what is now Pakistan.

Archaeologists have dug up thousands of clay tablets with writing on from all of those ancient places, so whether it first appeared on Harappan seals, Egyptian tombs or Sumerian pottery may always remain a mystery.

But without writing, where would Book be?

I like to think

of clay tablets as my ancestors.

Yes, I'll have you know that fired earth is part of Book's family tree, for clay tablets weren't just used to keep business records, lists and accounts. On clay tablets the Sumerians also stored secrets about the stars, as well as prayers, hymns and poems, and what's said to be the oldest story ever written down.

And what did they use for a pen? A reed. This ancient way of writing is called cuneiform, which means "wedge-shaped", because they used a reed stylus with a wedge-shaped tip to press into the soft clay.

Sounds like hard work. You try writing on squishy lumps of clay. Then you've got to sun-dry the clay or bake it in a fire, and if it cracks, well, there goes your paper. But, of course, the Sumerians weren't short of clay for they lived on the banks of two great rivers.

Here on this shelf, centuries later, I often wonder what it would feel like to be a clay tablet stored in a jar with a poem or story inscribed on me, and then to be dug up thousands of years later by an archaeologist searching among ruins in some faraway desert. Yes, I enjoy a bit of daydreaming – don't we all?

Then I look around at my friends, paperbacks and hardbacks, all of us huddled together here on the shelves, and I say to myself, What's got into you, Book? Your paper pages would go all brown and crunchy in the heat of the desert.

Your life

is a piece of clay;

don't let anyone else

mould it for you.

LAO TZU (c.604–c.531 BC)
Chinese philosopher

Before writing,
how did people manage

to send messages to each other across distances? Well, you could use a talking drum, or even send an object or two.

This might sound like a good idea, but it could be risky. In fact, I'll tell you about a moment in history when people got their frogs crossed. The story goes that when King Darius of Persia invaded Scythia, a messenger brought him a package from the Scythians.

In the package was a frog, a mouse, a bird and three arrows. Darius took this to mean that the Scythians were ready to surrender their land and retreat like birds before the Persian arrows.

But he had got the wrong end of the stick, or should that be the wrong end of the frog? What the Scythians were really saying to Darius was, "Look, mate, we Scythians aren't about to give up our land. So unless you Persians can hide like a frog in the swamps, burrow like a mouse or fly like a bird, you'd better not think about invading. Our Scythian arrows will get you, that's what."

Imagine going to all the trouble of catching a frog, a mouse, a bird – and still not getting your message across to the Persians! Surely, there had to be a better way of communicating.

Well, for starters, you could send a picture of a frog. At least then you wouldn't have to go hunting for a real one.

And once people began sending pictures, they realized they could use them to represent all sorts of things, not only objects or goods, like barley or cattle, but ideas.

If your message meant war, you could carve an arrow or a spear on a clay tablet and send that to your enemies.

If your message was wishing someone a long life, you could carve a snake, since there was an old belief that snakes lived for ever because they're always changing their old skin for a new one.

A picture of a foot might stand for, excuse the pun, the idea of a journey. Much like a roadside picture of an adult and child is part of modern traffic language, meaning watch out for children crossing.

Whether carved on clay, bark, ivory or bone, the arrival of picture writing or pictographs was a big step towards the miracle of the alphabet and yours truly, Book.

Down
the Alphabet Road

ᗡ ᐯ Ɛ Ⴧ Ⴈ

Picture-writing

techniques lived on in

the ancient Egyptian system of writing.
This was called hieroglyphics – a strange
word that means "sacred writing",
because it was mainly priests who had
access to this holy database.

There were over two thousand hiero-
glyphic characters, so it's no wonder
that they were surrounded in mystery,

and that it took archaeologists years to figure them all out.

But in the land of the pharaohs there also lived another people called the Phoenicians. Some of them were soldiers in the Egyptian army; some were miners looking for turquoise under the desert. They borrowed symbols from Egyptian hieroglyphics but made a big leap forward towards the alphabet as we know it today. Whereas the Egyptians used pictures to stand for things and ideas, the Phoenicians used pictures to stand for the actual sounds of spoken language.

Those Phoenicians were onto something that would send ripples across time and space, and that something was the alphabet. The ABC to me and you. The alphabet meant people wouldn't have to remember all the thousands of symbols used in hieroglyphics and more people would have a chance of learning to read and write.

Soon the alphabet was sailing the Mediterranean Sea, for the Phoenicians were great sailors and traders, and part of their cargo was a newly discovered export – the **ABC.**

That's why I, Book, would like to salute the Phoenicians, not just for the beautiful purple dye they exported, known as Phoenician purple, but also for phonetics, which is the study of the sounds of human speech.

"Of course you know your **ABC**?" said the Red Queen.

"To be sure I do," said Alice.

"So do I," the White Queen whispered. "We'll often say it over together, dear. And I'll tell you a secret – I can read words of one letter! Isn't *that* grand? However, don't be discouraged. You'll come to it in time."

LEWIS CARROLL *(1832–98)*
Through the Looking-Glass
English children's writer
and mathematician

TWEAKING
THE ABC

And so
the ABC took off.

Soon the ancient Greeks were coming up
with their own alphabet of twenty-two
letters. Alpha, beta, gamma, all the way
down to omega. No prizes for guessing
where the word "alphabet" comes from.
The Greeks also added their own vowel
letters, since the Phoenician language
only had consonants.

Enter

A E I O U

ά ἒ ἰ ὀ ὐ

It must have been fun being a little letter in those days, with different people taking you and shaping you to their own language. Straightening you here, curving you there, as they saw fit. Even writing you in all directions, right to left, left to right, not to mention downwards and upwards. A page must have felt like a trampoline.

And that's just what different ancient peoples – the Greeks, the Etruscans and the Romans – did with letters: they tweaked them to suit their language.

Now, when you write in English, you're using letters inherited from the Romans. But don't forget that those letters are the great-grandchildren of the Phoenician alphabet.

Once I get started on the subject of alphabets I could go on for ever. So let me ask you something instead. Do you like myths? Do you like brain-teasers? Well, try this:

What do the Egyptian god Thoth, the Greek god Hermes, the Norse god Odin and the Irish god Ogma have in common?

They all invented some form of alphabet.

For the Sumerians, it was their goddess Nisaba who passed on the gift of ancient cuneiform writing.

In India the goddess Sarasvati brought the Hindus the alphabet, and in her heart there is a special place for Book. During her festival, I always find myself next to prayer beads and white lotus flowers before her altar, and on this day young children write their first letter: the first letter of the Sanskrit alphabet:

Aum.

To see me

sitting quietly on this shelf,
waiting for someone to come along and browse through my pages, you'd never think I had a rock and rolling past, would you?

Let me make myself clear.

I say "rock" because whenever I see drawings done on the walls of caves by human hands more than thirty thousand years ago, I feel as if I'm gazing into rock illustrations of an ancient part of myself.

As for rolling – oh, you should have seen me in my rolling days! By then I was made of papyrus – a kind of paper – and wrapped around rolling rods. You might have thought Book was a roller blind or a roll of wallpaper. You'd hold me in one hand and, with the other, you'd be rolling me in order to read me. Sometimes, if I was many metres long, you'd even have to lay me on the floor and roll me along as you read.

I did some rolling in my time, I can tell you. I rolled in Europe until the Middle Ages. I rolled for longer in the Islamic world, where my letters were embossed in gold. And during that time I met rolls that had travelled all

the way from Asia. I guessed this from their picture-like Chinese writing, and I later learnt they were sacred Buddhist texts, made of birch bark, that had to be unrolled just like me.

I didn't have a spine yet. I'd lie spineless in my pigeonhole, my title on a little wooden tag, and I'd be rolled up and stored in a container like a big fat tube.

What was the reason for all this rolling? Simple. I had no pages to flip. At that time, Book took the form of scrolls, so to be precise, I should have said my *scrolling* days. But rolling days will do nicely. You can't take the roll out of the scroll, can you?

As a matter of fact, in these hi-tech times, when you read me on your electronic screen, you're back to

(sc)rolling

downwards or upwards as you read. Funny old world, isn't it?

Now let me

tell you a bit more about papyrus.
Thanks to that reedy plant growing in the swamps by the River Nile, I shed my old skin of clay and took on a new look and feel. You could call it my "Papyrus Period".

The Egyptians, you see, had found that by joining together flattened stalks of the papyrus plant, they could make a sort of paper to write on.

And they got very good value out of papyrus, I can tell you. They drank it, ate it, wore it, even sailed in it, and then they wrote on it.

Soon everyone who wrote used papyrus for writing on, and I was scrolling myself across many Mediterranean lands.

The Greeks called papyrus *byblos* because they imported it from a city port called Byblos. And that's why someone who can't resist the temptation of a bookshop is called a bibliophile or even, in extreme cases, a bibliomaniac.

The one problem with papyrus was that it couldn't be folded like today's paper. So though I looked beautiful, I was easily breakable. I was almost as brittle as dead leaves, and if it hadn't been for the dry climate of Egypt, I wouldn't have survived.

But survive I did.

And I must say, I had some exciting papyrus adventures. My favourite was when I was sealed in earth jars to accompany the dead on their journey to the underworld. Honest. I, Book, have lain beside mummies in Egyptian tombs, and trust me, you couldn't ask for a better travelling companion to the underworld than a mummy.

No wonder some people think that undertakers might have been the first book dealers.

And by the way, did you know that the word "paper" comes from the word "papyrus"? Just thought I'd mention it.

How Sheep Entered My Life

I was
still rolling when,

out of the blue, sheep entered my life. That's right. Deep down inside of me, there's a part that still bleats, especially when I daydream of days gone by, two thousand years ago and more, when a certain Ptolemy V, pharaoh of Egypt, took great pride in his library at Alexandria.

The story goes that when news reached him that King Eumenes II of Pergamum was buying up large quantities of papyrus and hoped to equal Alexandria's collection of over half a million scrolls, Ptolemy was having none of it. He gave orders that no more papyrus be exported from Egypt to Pergamum, a city port in Asia Minor.

But the king of Pergamum wasn't about to give up so easily. Necessity, they say, is the mother of invention, and Eumenes in turn gave orders that something must be found to take the place of papyrus. So after thinking long and hard, the people of Pergamum came up with an idea. Sheepskin. Without the woolly bits.

So there you have it. Now you know how sheep became part of my family tree. Sheepskin was the new papyrus. And this new writing material from the skin of the sheep of Pergamum would become known as parchment.

The skins of other animals such as cows and goats were also used in some places. And there's a very special kind of parchment called vellum. Makes you think of veal, did you say? Spot on. That's because vellum was made from the skin of a calf. I can't help feeling sorry for all the poor animals. It could take at least two hundred sheep to make one Bible, so just think how many it must have taken to make a whole library.

But if I'm honest, I was pleased with

= 1 **Bible**

my parchment and vellum look. I don't mean to sound vain, but you'd never believe how pampered I was in those days. After smoothing my roughness with a pumice stone, people would actually anoint my parchment skin with cedar oil to protect me from moth attacks.

Papyrus was still around, mind you, but since parchment wasn't as fragile as papyrus, my parchment look soon caught on.

SPREADING THE WORD
WITH FEATHERS

Centuries later,

monks were still copying me
on parchment in the monasteries of
Europe, using a goose quill for a pen
and a bull's horn for an inkwell, a
penknife on standby for scraping away
any mistakes.

So how would you like to be a monk
back in the Middle Ages and have to
pluck your pen from a bird?

Don't look so surprised. Back then,
people wrote with quill pens made
from the feathers of various birds.
Swan feathers were much prized for

their quality, turkey feathers for their strength, crow feathers for providing a fine nib.

No one asked the birds for their opinion, of course, but goose quills, which were the most popular, were in use until the nineteenth century, when the fountain pen was invented.

Did you know that when the English poet Edmund Spenser died in 1599, his fellow poets said farewell by dropping goose quills in his grave at Westminster Abbey?

And what do the wizards in Harry Potter write with? Quill pens.

As for going back to the Middle Ages, I must warn you that there was no popping to the shop to buy a bottle of ink. You had to pick gall apples, those small nutty brown balls that grow on oak trees – watch out for gall wasps! Then grind the gall apples up and leave them soaking in a pot. And that was only the beginning of a long, complicated process before you ended up with that precious liquid known as ink.

Never mind the backaching hours that went into preparing the parchment – another complicated business that meant soaking sheepskin or calfskin in lime water, and then leaving the slippery skins to dry.

Are you having second thoughts about going back to the Middle Ages? Too bad, because I'm taking you there!

When My Letters Shimmered

Imagine

yourself in a certain room
the monks called the Scriptorium. This
was where they spent devoted hours, even
in the darkness of winter; for no candle
was allowed, in case a precious page of
parchment or vellum got caught in the
flame and a scribe's handiwork that had
taken years was lost in moments.

Even in those dim stone rooms, you
can't imagine how Book glowed. You
could say it was Book's golden period
in the true sense of the word, for I was
in the more than capable hands of the
illuminators.

And who were these illuminators?

Mostly monks in monasteries, but also nuns in convents and professional artists.

And what exactly did these illuminators do?

Illuminate me.

With pictures that shone with colours from the juices of plants and made my pages come alive with the shimmer of gold and silver. So those who could not read and write would understand the meaning of stories from the Bible and the lives of the saints.

They worked for long hours in silence, until my parchment began to glow, each letter a soulful stroke.

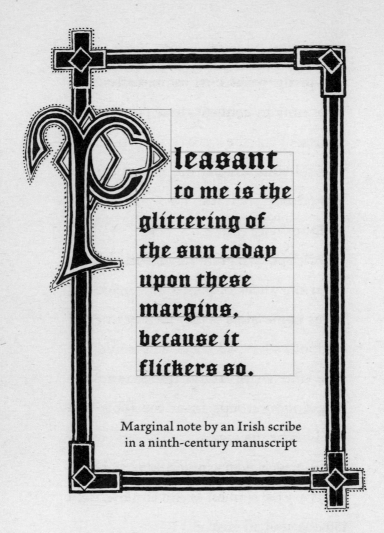

Pleasant to me is the glittering of the sun today upon these margins, because it flickers so.

Marginal note by an Irish scribe
in a ninth-century manuscript

This went on for hundreds of years, and great works of illuminated beauty were made behind those monastery walls, where the monks bent over me with their quill pens, copying me by hand, their red ink flowering in my margins.

Are you surprised to hear that in those days I was considered so precious I was kept under lock and key or even chained to a desk?

Well, I was. You don't know how lucky you are, dipping into me for free. And there you go, flipping my pages again! I can't help wondering what those monks and scribes would have had to say about that.

IF anyone steal this book, let him die the death. Let him be fried in the pan. Let the falling sickness and the fever seize him.

Let him be broken on the wheel, and hanged. ∞ Amen

Inscription in a twelfth-century Bible

Memories
of being handwritten

come back to me whenever I hear the word "manuscript". Do you know why a writer's work is called a manuscript, even when it's written on a computer? Because in the Latin language of the Romans "by hand" is *manu* and *scribo* means "I write".

And why do you think I am sometimes called Volume? Because those Romans rolled me up and down, and in Latin, the word *volvere* means ... wait for it ... "to roll". Makes you think of "revolve", doesn't it?

Strange creatures, words. The way they germinate like seeds.

Now I'd like to tell you about something those Romans did that changed my shape for ever. It must have been very awkward for them reading me and rolling me at the same time. So instead of pasting my parchment together end to end and rolling me, they started folding me up and binding me along my folds with leather thongs or strips of wood. And so I came to be called Codex, from their Latin word *caudex*, meaning "tree trunk".

With a wooden binding for a spine, I was handy and easier to carry. People didn't have to roll me. They could flip my pages backwards or forwards until they came to the one they were looking for. And now there was writing on both sides of my parchment, the front and the back. Not just on one side like in my papyrus days.

I can't tell you how exciting it was to be able to stand upright in pretty much the same rectangular shape you see me in to this day in a bookshop window or on a library shelf. Yes, I'm still standing in my codex form.

And do you know what? People are still flipping my pages when they want to find a favourite passage or poem. You'd think they'd have a look at my index or contents page first, but no, there's something about human fingers that can't seem to resist giving Book a good flip.

And I've got to admit, though I've never said this before, that when I feel my pages being flipped, a tingle of excitement runs down my spine. Is this person about to read me? I'm thinking. Or are they just flipping and dipping into me?

In case you hadn't noticed,

I have a soft spot for the letter

Now, don't get me wrong, I love all twenty-six letters of the alphabet. Without them, how would writers put all those long sentences inside me? But I'm not ashamed to admit I do have a special liking for P, a letter that reminds me of high moments in Book's life:

Papyrus.

Parchment.

Paper.

Printing Press.

Paperback.

Page.

Publisher.

See what I mean? That was just me, by the way, trying to make up a little Poem. Thought I'd give it a go.

And now I'm going to tell you about one of those high moments: the coming of paper. Not that my papyrus and parchment weren't kinds of paper, but I'm talking real paper, like the stuff you're holding right now.

Who invented paper? Who thought of making it from plant fibres and old rags? Given the chance, I would like to say a personal thank you to that person, who happened to be a Chinese scholar by the name of Ts'ai Lun.

If only he could flip my pages now, Ts'ai Lun would be ever so proud of what he gave to the world. But perhaps "gave" is too strong a word, for he didn't exactly say, "Hey, world, I've just invented paper; here's the recipe." No, it didn't happen quite like that.

The story goes that, one day, he came up with the idea of pounding bamboo and mulberry bark into a pulp. He then mixed the pulp with water, strained it through a cloth and left it to dry in the sun. And from Ts'ai Lun's mushy mash – hey presto, paper was born.

That was nearly two thousand years ago. The secret of paper remained with the Chinese for hundreds of years. They wrote on it, made kites out of it, even used it for toilet paper, until the Arabs discovered the secret and took it with them to a place called Samarkand, then on to Spain in the twelfth century. Soon there were paper-making mills all over Europe.

By then the Aztecs in South America were also making paper, from fibres of the agave plant. And in exchange for Arab horses and camels, the sultans of Kashmir in India were offering fine Kashmir paper made from linen, flax and hemp rags.

Needless to say, I was delighted with this development. Some people still felt I looked more beautiful in parchment and vellum. But you can't please everybody, can you? And since they were so expensive, I thought, Paper's fine by me. In fact, I was happy to see the words in me reveal themselves in a mirror

a. Flax (Linum usitatissimum)

b. Bamboo (Dendrocalamus asper)

c. Cotton (Gossypium hirsutum)

d. Paper Mulberry
  (Broussonetia papyrifera)

e. Banana (Musa acuminata)

f. Hemp (Cannabis sativa)

g. Agave (Agave sisalana)

of paper. And quietly I said to myself,
Thank you, all you plants.

Talking of plants, if I tell you that
I'm related to the beech tree, you'll
probably think I'm kidding. Well, it
might interest you to know that once
upon a time, strips of beech were used
for writing on, so the old English word
boc means "beech" as well as "book".

And since paper comes from plants,
you could say that plants, like the clay

that once made me, are part of Book's breathing ancestry.

As a matter of fact, I'll have you know that I've been made from palm leaves in India, from mulberry leaves in Japan, from banana leaves in the Philippines. And don't you call my pages leaves? Don't you *speak* of leafing through my pages? And among Native Americans, wasn't I, Book, known as Talking Leaves?

I had often seen my master and
Dick employed in reading; and I
had a great curiosity to talk to the
books, as I thought they did; and
so to learn how all things had a
beginning: for that purpose I have
often taken up a book, and have
talked to it, and then put my ears
to it, when alone, in hopes it would
answer me; and I have been very
much concerned when I found it
remained silent.

Olaudah Equiano (c.1745–97)
*The Interesting Narrative of the Life of Olaudah
Equiano or Gustavus Vassa, the African*

Kidnapped aged eleven and transported into
slavery, Equiano learnt to read and write
and self-published his autobiography in 1789.
His book rapidly sold out and was reprinted
several times, while Equiano travelled across
Britain, lending his voice to the movement
to end slavery.

GUTENBERG'S MOVABLE TYPE

I was

over the moon

about the coming of paper, but even more exciting news was to come.

Something massive was in the air.

Something that would change me for ever.

It had already been happening in Korea, where people were using what's called movable type to print me. (This was in fact an invention borrowed from the Chinese, who, you'll remember, bless them, also came up with the idea of paper.)

Then in the fifteenth century news came from Germany that a goldsmith by the name of Johannes Gutenberg had found a way of printing letters of metal type onto a sheet of paper much faster than copying them by hand.

Not only that. Gutenberg was claiming that he could even rearrange and reuse those same letters to form new sentences.

It was the first time anyone in Europe had ever heard of printing. It sounded too good to be true, but it was happening for real. I was flying on the wings of Gutenberg's movable type.

Let us break the seal which seals up holy things and give wings to Truth in order that she may win every soul that comes into the world by her word no longer written at great expense by hands easily palsied, but multiplied like the wind by an untiring machine.

JOHANNES GUTENBERG
(c.1400–68)
German printer and inventor
of the Western printing press
using movable type

Now I could see myself on the printing press being multiplied

a hundredfold,

a thousandfold,

a millionfold.

With greater quantities of me being produced, I, Book, was getting cheaper, which meant more people could now afford to buy me. I didn't have to belong just to the rich or, for that matter, the monks and the nuns who were scribes. I could enter the minds and imaginations of poor people who were at last learning to read and write.

There is no Frigate like a Book

To take us lands away,

Nor any Coursers like a Page

Of prancing Poetry.

This Traverse may the poorest take

Without oppress of Toil;

How frugal is the Chariot

That bears a Human Soul!

EMILY DICKINSON *(1830–86)*
American poet

And because I had become much cheaper and easier to carry around, I began to spread ideas beyond borders. I, Book, became a portable bridge across time and space, a lighthouse shining in the sea of time, giving the light of my pages wherever there was hunger for the written word.

And here's something interesting: after the invention of the printing press, the price of reading glasses went down because more people were reading.

Today you'll see the printed word everywhere. On billboards. On posters. On the newspaper headline spotted out of the corner of your eye and the junk mail pouring through your letter box.

Thanks to print, readers by their thousands could now own an identical copy of me. I wouldn't want to upset any scientists out there, but you could say the printed Book was the world's first positive clone.

Of course, there were those who were still suspicious and considered the printing press to be the work of the devil. But was I complaining? Not in the least. Print put Book at the very cutting edge of change.

THE famine of books will be at an end. All nations will be able to acquire books at low cost.

What glory for our Empire, and what prayers for its perpetuity will be made, when they see so many good books which communicate knowledge to them, of which till then they had been destitute.

This motive alone should suffice for our Invincible Emperor to protect and permit the establishment of printing.

IBRAHIM MUTEFERRIKA (C.1674–1745)
Hungarian-born scholar and diplomat
of the Ottoman Empire, he introduced
printing to Turkey.

Looking back,

I can see why the nineteenth century, the age of steam power, has also been called the golden age of print. For it was steam that powered the new press invented in 1814 by Friedrich Koenig, a German like Gutenberg.

Gutenberg's press had been around for more than three hundred years, when Koenig found a way of using steam instead of hands to operate a printing press. This meant books could be printed far more quickly, and that was good news for the printed word, and of course good news for Book.

I was being produced at such a rate, I could hardly keep up with myself and all the other changes that were happening around me.

Daily newspapers were spreading far and wide, as the steam press made them faster and cheaper to print. And with more and more people learning to read and write, the future looked bright.

But there were more changes to come.

By the middle of the century I was used to being mass-produced on the steam press, when I found myself being rolled off it at greater speed than ever before.

I later learnt that an American inventor, Richard Hoe, was behind this new development. The rotary press, as it was called, was the closest I've come to a roller-coaster ride.

Luckily, I'd had my share of rolling in my papyrus days – but the rotary press brought rolling to a new level. I'll spare you the technical details, but I remember being on cylinders shaped like big drums and whirling on ink-rollers that were fed by what seemed a never-ending stream of rolled-up paper.

What a thrill it was to watch my printed pages rolled off at high speed! I couldn't help thinking back to a certain Bi Sheng, the Chinese vendor who first came up with the idea of movable type. His clay and porcelain pieces had been replaced with metal ones, but his idea of movable type was alive and well in the printing presses invented a thousand years later.

Soon

printing houses

were springing up all over Europe. New ideas and movements were in the air, and in my printed form I was reaching out to those who for generations had been held captive by old systems of political and religious beliefs.

I guess you've heard of the **Reformation**, a movement that set out to reform the old Roman Catholic Church, which had held power for centuries. Well, it came as no surprise to me that it began in Germany, home of the first printing press. You could even say the

Reformation was the child of print, and print was the fairy godmother to Book.

By the beginning of the seventeenth century, I was busy doing something else too: opening up new continents of the imagination. I was stirring up a rebirth – a **Renaissance** of interest in ancient cultures.

By simply looking inside me at old drawings and texts from ancient Greek and Roman times, artists, scientists, architects, philosophers, poets and novelists found ideas and inspiration.

It was the beginning of what's called the **Enlightenment**, and it would never have happened without yours truly. I like to think that it was I, Book, who enlightened the Enlightenment, if you know what I mean.

Because how else would scientists have learnt of all the ideas and all the discoveries that led them to invent amazing new machines in the middle of the eighteenth century?

The greatest discovery of that hundred-year **Industrial Revolution** was the power of steam. And take it from me, Book was there.

How well I remember the day in 1825 when the first public steam railway was opened up. Oh, the excitement of sitting on a passenger's lap and feeling my pages being turned, and the pride rushing down my spine, as the steam engine puffed its way through the countryside of northern England.

Where the rail tracks were leading, I couldn't say. But I know we were speeding past wagons drawn by horses.

The locomotive was on the move.

And so was Book.

A Garden in a Pocket

Fast-forward

a hundred years, and I had witnessed even more changes in myself and around me, including one world war that had brought millions great suffering. Yet the centuries seemed to have gone by in the twinkle of an eye or, should I say, the flip of a page.

It's as if one day I was being rolled and scrolled, then suddenly I had a spine and a proper hardback cover, made from cardboard or leather. Not to mention a removable dust jacket, complete with foldable flaps, in case you hadn't noticed.

And on my dust jacket is where

you'll find something called a blurb that tells you briefly what I'm about. Funny word, blurb! Apparently it was invented by the American writer Gelett Burgess who, at a booksellers' meeting in 1907, promoted his latest work with a special cover. On it was a picture of a smiling lady called Belinda Blurb saying nice things about his book. The idea caught on, and that's why to this day the blurb on my dust jacket says positive things about my contents. (And a nice word or two about the writer doesn't go amiss either!)

Years later, with another world war looming, I began to fear for the future. Not again, I thought. Not more people screaming under clouds of grief. And what would become of Book? I had heard talk of paper being in short supply, even of bombs dropped on warehouses where millions like me were stored.

But before that I was to experience yet another change. Something happened to the stitches and staples in my binding. How strange, I thought. Well, wouldn't you be surprised, if you were accustomed to being a hardback, to suddenly find yourself a paperback?

Now I was held together with glue, and my paper back made it easy to carry me in a pocket or slip me into a handbag. Today you'll find me equally at home on a revolving rack at a train station or at an airport, but back in the late 1930s I was just getting used to the paperback feeling, as people experimented with soft covers in America, Germany and England.

And when the Second World War came, amid all the hopelessness, unrest and sadness, many a soldier tucked me into his breast pocket. I was his paperback companion on that terrible journey. I, Book, hand-held witness to his final hour.

But I mustn't dwell on the bad times. Let me just say how pleased I was to be a paperback. My hardback look wasn't about to disappear, but my paperback look caught on with publishers around the world and the growing reading public.

And people carried me everywhere. On trains, on buses. They slipped me into their picnic baskets, and sometimes – dare I say – I even accompanied them into their bath. Yes, I have experienced the odd sprinkle of bubbles across my paperback face.

Book had come a long way from being chained to a desk.

And believe me, it felt good to be so portable. Not only was I a carrier of the imagination, influencing the world of ideas, but I could be carried across continents in a bag or a briefcase.

Wasn't it the Chinese who compared me to a garden in a pocket? I like the sound of that.

The books I love

are well fingered and thumbed

have tiny butter smudges

may harbour a crumb

the odd cat-whisker

a few dog-ears

a drop of tear

a brownish stain

(that looks suspiciously like tea)

I for one, am glad to say,

do not judge a book

by its cover —

but flit first among its leaves

like a hummingbird

sipping at a flower

The books I love

I must admit do not sit

behind a museum of glass.

No the books I love

get kissed and squeezed

and pressed against my heart.

GRACE NICHOLS *(1950–)*
"Book-heart"
Guyanese-British poet

THE HOUSE OF MEMORY

But what

about people who wanted

to read but couldn't afford to buy me?

Well, as you know, there was and still is a place where you can borrow me for free and take me home, though if you keep me too long you have to pay what's called overdues.

Such a place was called the "house of memory" by the Sumerians, "the healing place of the soul" by the Egyptians, and "an ocean of gems" by the Tibetans.

I'm talking about a library, of course.

As far back as I can remember, there were libraries. They grew as writing grew. Ages ago a librarian was known as a "keeper of tablets" and a library as the "house of tablets". Takes me back to the days of writing on clay. One Assyrian king I knew then was such a keen collector of clay tablets, he even had his own library with a built-in kiln for baking them. Talk about hot off the press!

I've been in libraries in the palaces of Egyptian pharaohs, going all the way back to my scrolling days in Alexandria.

I've been in libraries in Roman baths.

By then I was in my hand-held codex form with a binding of wood, and I can tell you, those Romans sure knew how to mix their bathing with their browsing.

I've been in libraries in Indian temples as treasured writings on palm leaves, and even in bone libraries. You heard me. Bone libraries. That was when I was in China, where they wrote on the bones of oxen and tortoise shells.

Most memorable of all, I've been to Timbuktu, where I saw the Tuareg nomads, and, like them, I journeyed on the backs of camels. What I remember most about that sub-Saharan city was its ancient desert library and the sight of university scholars kissing fragile manuscripts gilded in Arabic calligraphy.

Now that you've got me started on libraries, let me tell you about the time I nearly drowned. Can I swim? What a silly question! Once, I was on a floating library, going down a river in Asia. The Ganges, to be exact. It was during the long monsoon season, and I was heading to a far-flung village. Since the rains had stopped the people from getting to a library, the library was going to them.

Suddenly I found myself overboard. If I had been made of papyrus, like in the old days, I might have stood a chance. For didn't little Moses go floating down the Nile in a basket made of papyrus rushes? At least, so I heard. But there I was, all printed and hardbound, quite a heavy volume, and I thought, It's the bottom of the river for you, Book. Start saying your prayers.

I was wearing my laminated jacket, but even so, after a brief float, not exactly the breaststroke, I was about to sink. Luckily the goddess of learning, Sarasvati herself, must have been watching over me. In the nick of time, some librarian's hand plucked me from the water and dried me out, page by tender loving page.

And so I, Book, a born survivor, lived to tell a tale of water as I would one day live to tell a tale of flames.

I have always imagined Paradise to be a kind of library.

JORGE LUIS BORGES *(1899–1986)*
Argentinian poet
and essayist

Open to the Public

Did you know

that even though there were
libraries in Rome as early as the first
century AD, it wasn't until the middle
of the nineteenth century that libraries
were opened to the general public for
free? Before then they belonged to royal
households, monasteries, cathedrals and
universities.

Nowadays, all you need is that
magical thing called a library ticket,
and a library is no longer a hush-hush
place for the wealthy.

Sitting on my shelf, I listen in to
storytellers telling stories, and novelists

and poets reading aloud from their work and saying what inspired them. I see illustrators doing drawings right there in front of wide-eyed schoolchildren on cushions. I even hear the children joining in and clapping, till I feel like clapping my own pages.

But I can remember the days when there was a sign outside libraries:

NO CHILDREN OR DOGS ALLOWED.

How times change.

Now libraries are for everyone, and what really makes my day is when I give pleasure to the elderly who come to have a read or just to keep warm and enjoy a bit of company. Those ancient Greeks knew what they were talking about when they called a library the "medicine chest of the soul".

It's a bit different today, of course, because I can see stacks of DVDs and computer screens staring at me from my shelf. Sometimes I feel like saying, "What are you looking at?" But I mustn't be rude, even though I'm a little disappointed when someone puts me

It was from my own early experience that I decided there was no use to which money could be applied so productive of good to boys and girls who have good within them and ability and ambition to develop it, as the founding of a public library.

ANDREW CARNEGIE *(1835–1919)*
A very, very rich Scottish American
industrialist who used his money
to fund over two and a half thousand
free libraries across the world.

back on the shelf and decides to borrow a DVD instead.

Never mind. I, Book, know how to be patient. One day a hand will reach for me and take me to the counter to be stamped. Checked out and, we hope, returned.

When politicians talk about closing a library to save money, I feel like knocking them over the head. And my hardback spine can give a jolly hard knock, I can tell you.

Ah, libraries. Where would I be without them? Having said that, where would they be without me? They are my orchard; I am their fruit.

I entered an orchard
where the fruits could be eaten
yet returned to the tree.

I sat in a garden
where the flowers could be picked
yet no harm come to the stems.

I went into a house
that was empty of people
yet peopled with voices.

I was in a room
that hadn't much of a view
yet horizons leaned towards me.

In this place – I forgot myself
in ancient memory
yet found myself renewed.

Where was I? A library.

JOHN AGARD (1949–)
"In This Place"
Guyanese-British poet

A Tale of Flames

I said

earlier that I have lived

to tell a tale of flames. Though you may find this part of my life disturbing, I'll tell it all the same, for, as the saying goes, history sadly repeats itself.

Let me take you back over two thousand years to ancient China, the very birthplace of paper and printing. There I was burnt along with scholars who were buried beside me.

The man who gave the order was the same emperor who built the famous wall that stretches five thousand miles and more on China's border. Little did he know that imagination has no walls. And that while he was building a great wall, I, Book, was building great bridges between one mind and another.

And isn't it ironic that I was also burnt by people who, through their religious faith, have been called "people of the Book"?

Believe me, I have been destroyed by hands that considered themselves holy. They threw me to the flames as they would later throw women whose wisdom was beyond theirs and whom they called witches.

In the Andean highlands of South America in the sixteenth century, was I not burnt by Spanish priests? They couldn't understand Mayan pictograms, and what they did not understand they considered dangerous.

During the Second World War, was I not burnt by the Nazis in Europe's Germany, the very place that had seen the light of Gutenberg's movable type?

> *Wherever they burn books they will also, in the end, burn human beings.*
>
> **HEINRICH HEINE** *(1797–1856)*
> German poet of Jewish origin

And was I not burnt, along with over a million others, when Serbian soldiers set fire to the National Library of Sarajevo in 1992? Anyone who tried to save us risked being shot.

And while the flames of war were rising in Iraq, was not Baghdad's ancient library also burning? There, between those great rivers, the Tigris and Euphrates, believed by many to be the cradle of early writing, my blackened pages blew in the wind.

Wherever there is Book, there you will find the shadow of burning.

And when I think of such acts, although I myself am made of words, I am all of a sudden lost for words. I find, at moments like these, a poem says it best.

When the regime ordered that books with harmful knowledge

Should be publicly burnt, and all around

Oxen were forced to drag cartloads of books

To the pyre, one banished poet

One of the best, discovered, studying the list of the burnt

To his horror, that his books

Had been forgotten. He hurried to his desk

On wings of rage and wrote a letter to the powers that be.

Burn me! he wrote, his pen flying, burn me!

Don't do this to me! Don't pass me over! Have I not always told

The truth in my books? And now

I am treated by you as a liar!

I order you:

Burn me!

BERTOLT BRECHT *(1898–1956)*
"The burning of books"
German playwright and poet

Bertolt Brecht's words remind me that memory, like truth, will always find a witness. Somewhere in a dictator's dungeon, having no access to paper, or even a pencil, some hand will carve thoughts on a loaf of bread, on a bar of soap.

And from blank spaces, in soulless places, I will blossom into Book, scattering my seeds across the shelves of the imagination.

The paper burns,

but the words fly away.

AKIBA BEN JOSEPH (C. AD 50–135)
Palestinian rabbi

1 Book eBook

Are my pages
a rustle of the past?

Will I gather dust on the shelf? Am I, Book, about to be for ever eBook?

Let me answer by beginning, as they say, at the beginning.

Do you believe in evolution? Maybe you do; maybe you don't. But by eBook you mean electronic book, right?

Well, for me, when I think eBook, I'm thinking e-volving book. You know, if Darwin were still around, he might at this minute be tracing my descent and giving my family tree odd names like *Bookus papyrus* and *Bookus paperbackus* and now *Bookus electronicus*.

I don't need Darwin to tell me that my crumpable skin is mutating onto a screen. But it gives a new twist to the process of natural selection, doesn't it?

Now you can download me, upload me, toggle me on something called an iPad, Kindle me, google me, even blog me. Makes the mind bloggle, doesn't it?

How will I cope with this digital environment?

Well, you know what I'm like. I'm a survivor. I've witnessed countless mindless burnings – do you really think a bit of cyberspace is going to scare me?

The way I see it, I suppose, is rather philosophical.

When I was made of papyrus,
wasn't I **vegetable?**

When I was made of ivory,
wasn't I **mineral?**

When I was made of sheepskin,
wasn't I **animal?**

I guess you could call me
elemental.

So here I come, **digital.**

The other day, I happened to be on a table near a young eBook. It was one of those unexpected meetings. Anyway, you know what youth is like. There he was, making his flickering screen prance up and down, showing off what he called his hypertext.

So I said, "Better not get too *high-per*, because when your battery needs charging, you'll come crashing down, won't you?"

That didn't go down too well.

Now, don't get me wrong. I have lots of friends who happen to be eBooks. They tell me they're saving the rainforest by saving paper, and I can't argue with that.

They also say that readers with

certain physical disabilities find it easier to thumb a menu button than thumb my pages. That's a point. There's a lot to be said for that. I can see where they're coming from.

But I had to speak up for myself. I couldn't very well let eBook do all the talking, could I? So to show that I was used to change, I pointed out that since Louis Braille's invention to help the blind to read, I've seen my pages seeded with tiny raised dots, making it possible for millions of blind people to read me.

"Don't talk to me about change," I said to eBook. "I can tell you a thing or two about change. Haven't I witnessed centuries of it, from the birth of the

Braille is knowledge,
and knowledge is power.

LOUIS BRAILLE *(1809–52)*

Born in France and blinded when he
was three by a knitting needle,
Louis Braille went on at the age
of seventeen to create a system of
reading by raised dots.

alphabet to being handwritten with a stylus, then a quill, right through to that great leap into print?

"And long before your time, I was typed on a machine called a typewriter. You weren't even a pixel in a screen's twinkle! Writers thought typewriters were the bee's knees and loved to hear their words

tap-dancing

through the space of the blank page."

I will now claim — until dispossessed — that I was the first person in the world to apply the typewriter to literature...

That early machine was full of caprices ... devilish ones.

MARK TWAIN *(1835–1910)*
American writer.
His novel *Tom Sawyer* was written
on a Remington typewriter.

Then suddenly, out of the blue, I blurted, "Anyway, I smell nicer than you."

eBook looked puzzled. "Smell? What exactly is smell? Do books smell?"

"Where have you been, eBook?" I said. "Of course books smell. Have you never heard the expression 'nose in a book'?"

DO YOU KNOW THAT BOOKS SMELL LIKE NUTMEG OR SOME SPICE FROM A FOREIGN LAND? I LOVED TO SMELL THEM WHEN I WAS A BOY.

RAY BRADBURY *(1938–2012)*
American writer

And I told eBook about Roman times, when my vellum smelt of saffron, and Victorian times, when my paper smelt of pressed lavender and rose petals.

I was quick to point out that not all books smell the same, of course; but a well-trained nose, like a keen wine taster, can pick up a hint of mature wood pulp tinged with vanilla, as if the forest itself had stamped me with the smell of ancient wisdom.

I let eBook know in no uncertain terms that my old musty smell is a heart-warming perfume to the nose of book lovers rummaging in second-hand shops, car boot sales, charity shops and what have you.

This year for the first time
I've actually bought more eBooks
than printed books. A couple
of years ago I would have sworn
that it could never happen.
My house already contains around
15,000 printed books but I now
reluctantly admit that books
I know I'm only ever going to read
once are bought in electronic form.
If it's a book I'll want to return
to again and again, then
the printed book rules.

MALORIE BLACKMAN *(1962–)*
English writer and Children's Laureate

Then I changed the subject and told him it was a shame he couldn't experience the thrill of being dog-eared. That shut him up.

He said he had to love me and leave me because his battery needed charging. He also said something about having to be booted up. I didn't like the sound of that. Whatever happened to a good flip of the page with that thing called a thumb?

But to this day eBook and I are good friends, though every now and then I have to remind him that an old codex like me has been around for hundreds of years. And I have no immediate plans to become extinct.

Reading off the screen is still vastly inferior to reading off paper. Even I, who have these expensive screens and fancy myself as a pioneer of this Web Lifestyle, when it comes to something over about four or five pages, I print it out and I like to have it to carry around with me and annotate. And it's quite hard for technology to match that level of usability.

BILL GATES *(1955–)*
Former Microsoft chairman

I,
Book,

can't very well tell you

the story of my life without

saying a *thank you* from

the bottom of my spine

to all the people who make

me and care about me.

To

BIBLIOPHILES for collecting me

BOOKBINDERS for binding me

BOOKSELLERS for selling me

DESIGNERS for designing me

EDITORS for editing me

ILLUSTRATORS for illustrating me

LIBRARIANS for lending me

PRINTERS for printing me

READERS for reading me

REVIEWERS for reviewing me

(favourably or not)

TRANSLATORS for translating me

WRITERS for writing me

You'll notice that I mention writers last. No disrespect. That's what happens when you say things in what's called alphabetical order.

Next time I'll say "authors" instead of "writers", so authors come first. But they won't be too upset. Writers know that somewhere it is written that the first shall be last and the last shall be first.

What more can I say, dear Reader, except this? I am there for you.

You know where to find me – just ask for Book.

SOURCES

Not being a historian or a linguist, I had to ferret through a number of books and random sources, too numerous to mention. But my thanks to:

BLACK ON WHITE: THE STORY OF BOOKS
by M. Ilin (Routledge & Kegan Paul, 1932)

THE BOOK ON THE BOOKSHELF
by Henry Petroski (Vintage, 2000)

THE CASE FOR BOOKS: PAST, PRESENT AND FUTURE
by Robert Darnton (Public Affairs, 2010)

EX LIBRIS: CONFESSIONS OF A COMMON READER
by Anne Fadiman (Farrar, Straus and Giroux, 2000)

A HISTORY OF READING
by Alberto Manguel (Penguin Books, 1997)

MY SECRET PLANET
by Dennis Healey (Penguin Books, 1994)

THE STORY OF THE BOOK
by Agnes Allen (Faber and Faber, 1952)

My thanks also to the poets Bertolt Brecht, Emily Dickinson and Grace Nichols for the use of their poems in telling Book's story, and to Tom Eilenberg for his enthusiastic research.

ACKNOWLEDGEMENTS

The author and publishers gratefully acknowledge permission to use the following material:

"Book-heart" reproduced with permission of Curtis Brown Group Ltd, London on behalf of Grace Nichols, Copyright © 2006 Grace Nichols

"The burning of books" originally published in German in 1939 as "Die Bucherverbrennung". Copyright © 2014 by Thomas Mark Kuhn and David J. Constantine. Copyright © 1939 by Bertolt-Brecht-Erben/Suhrkamp Verlag, from *Collected Poems of Bertolt Brecht* by Bertolt Brecht, translated by Thomas Mark Kuhn and David J. Constantine. Used by permission of Liveright Publishing Corporation

Malorie Blackman copyright © Malorie Blackman. As published in *The Author* (Autumn, 2011), reproduced by permission

Every reasonable effort has been made to trace ownership of and/or secure permission for the use of copyrighted material. If notified of any omission, the author and publisher will gladly make the necessary correction in future printings.

JOHN AGARD is a poet, playwright and children's writer. He was born in Guyana. His many poetry collections include *We Brits, Alternative Anthem, Travel Light, Travel Dark* and *Goldilocks on CCTV*. He has co-edited a number of anthologies for children with his wife, the poet Grace Nichols. He has won several awards for his work, including the Queen's Gold Medal for Poetry in 2012.

NEIL PACKER graduated from Colchester School of Art and worked on advertising campaigns before illustrating *One Hundred Years of Solitude, The Name of the Rose* and *Labyrinths* for the Folio Society, and Gillian Cross's retellings of the *Odyssey* and *The Iliad* for Walker Books.